I0462349

FLIPBOOK

CLAUDE

CF

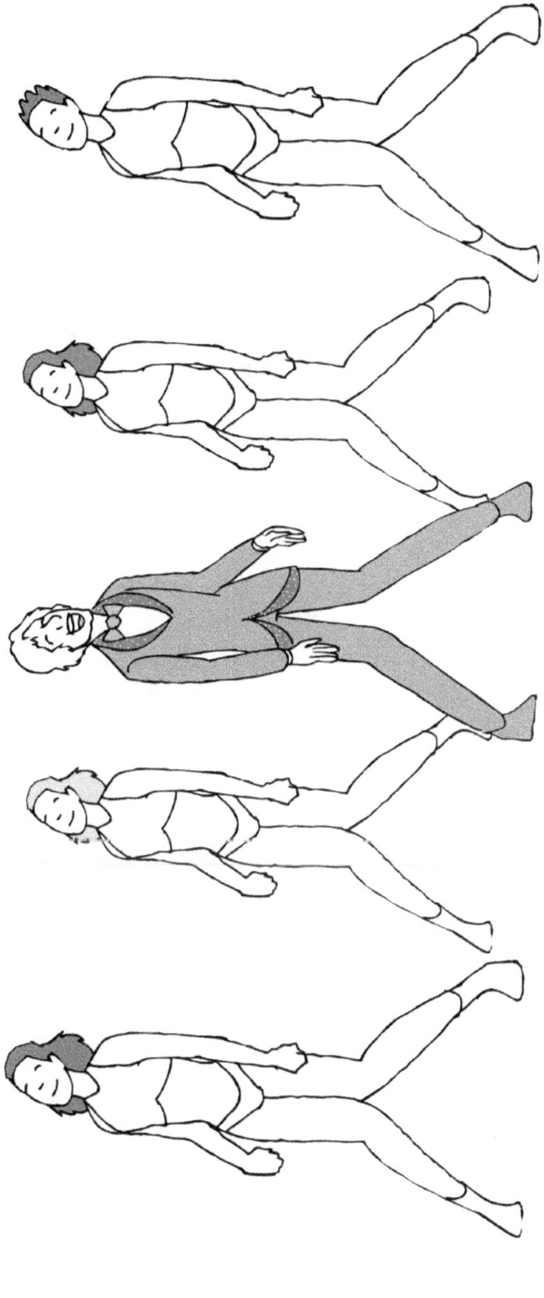

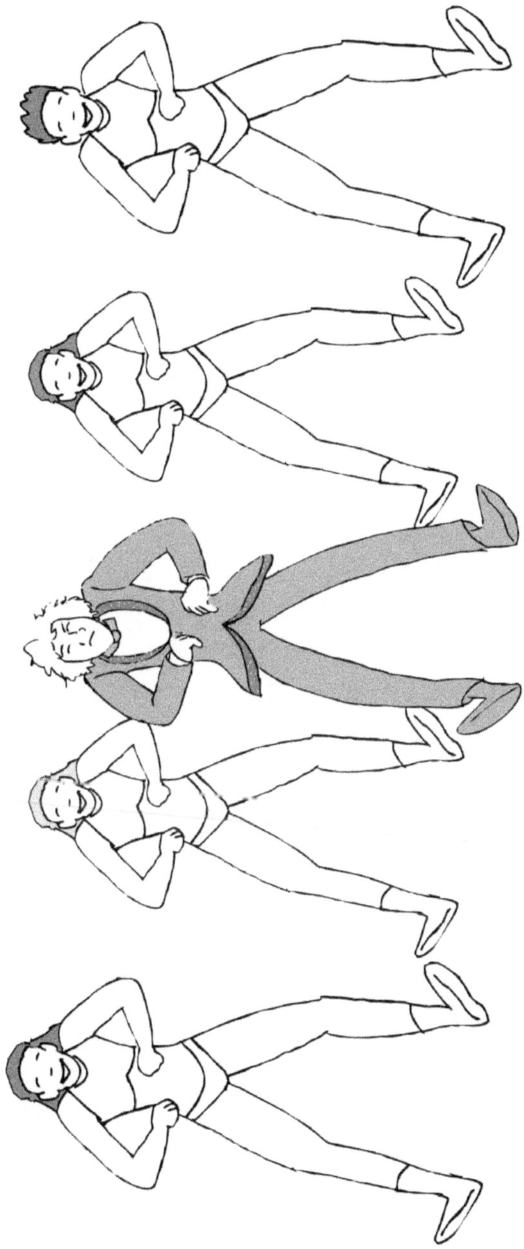

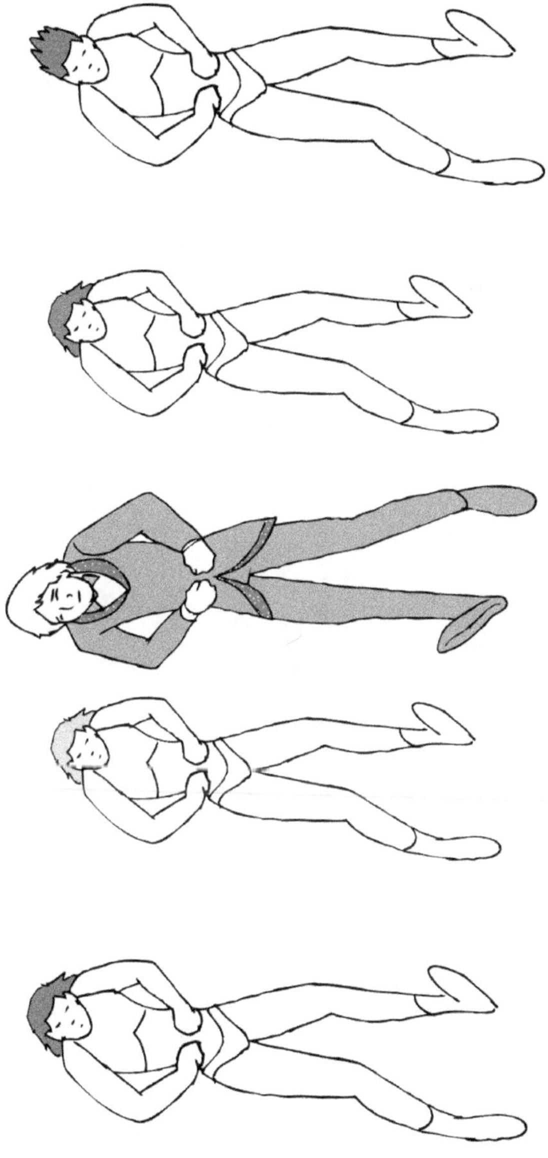

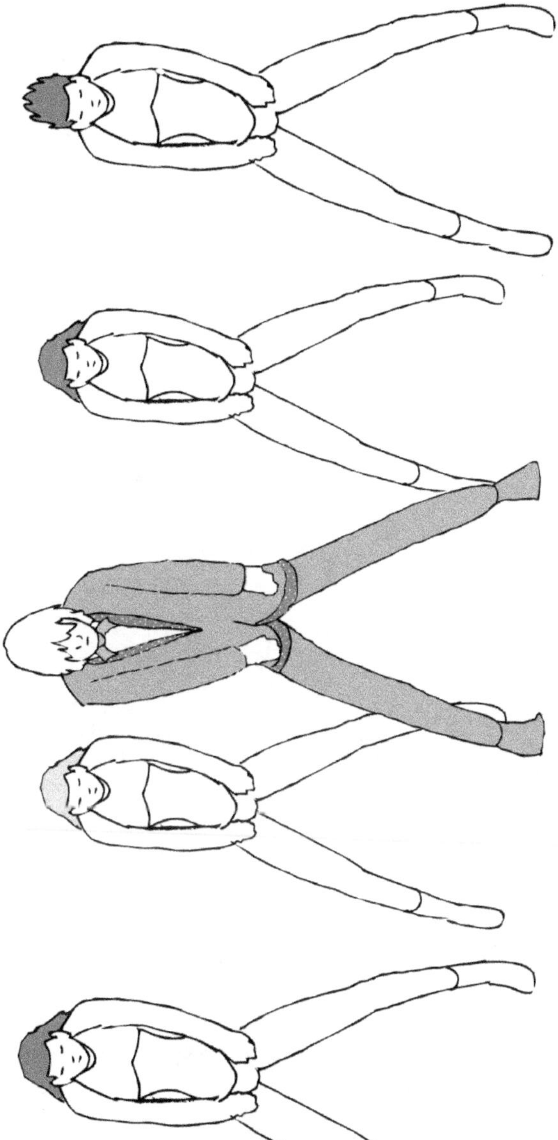

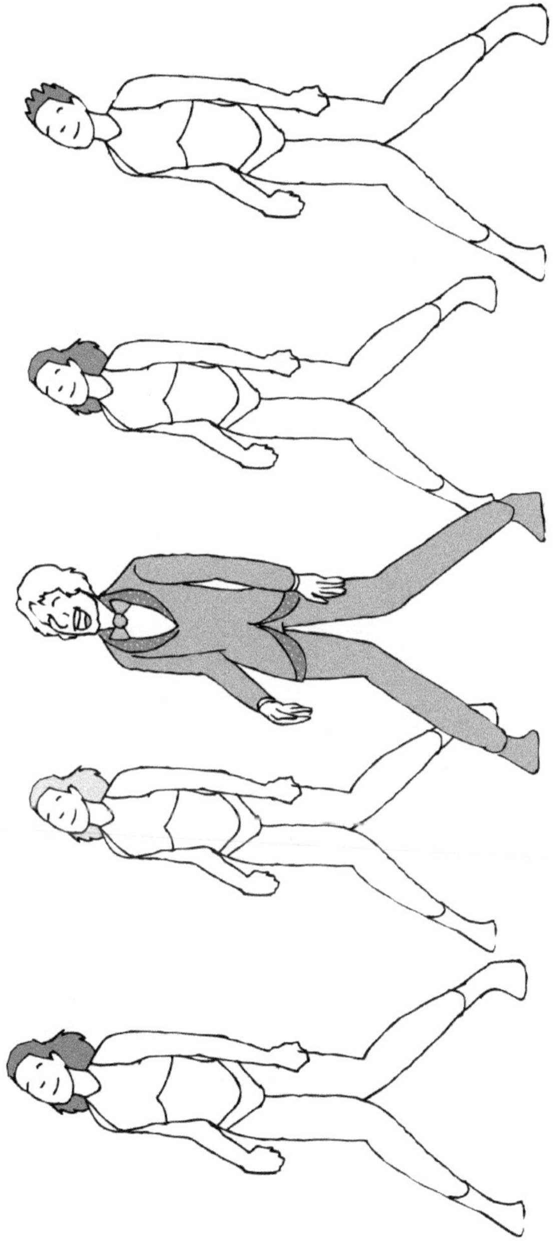

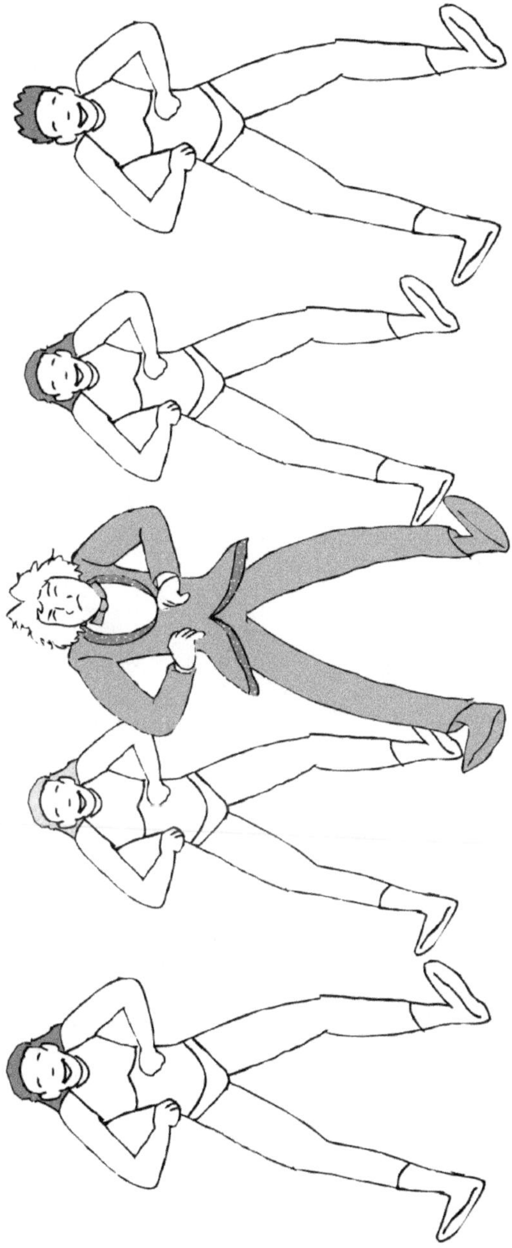

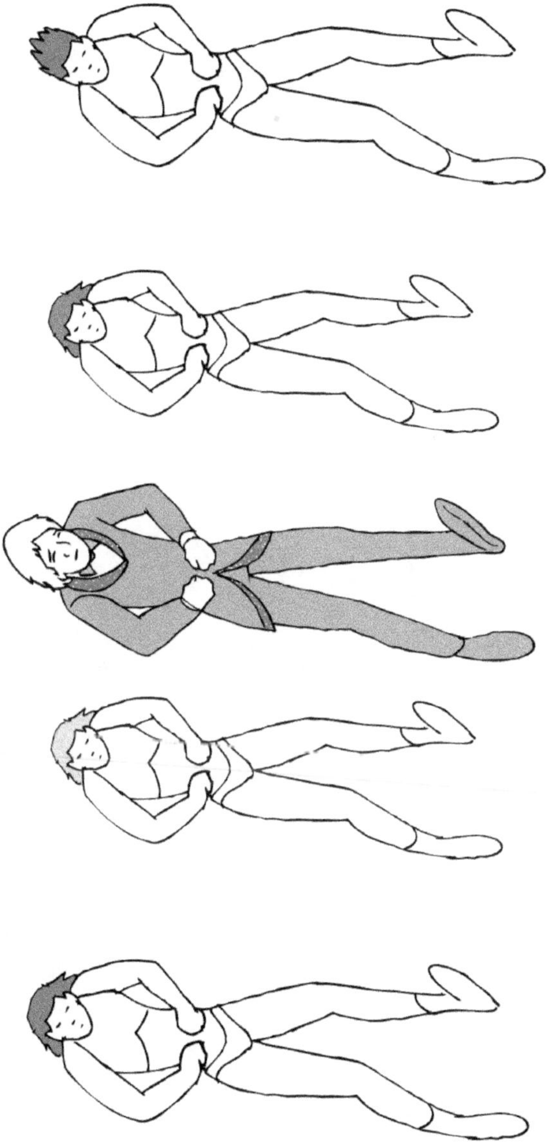

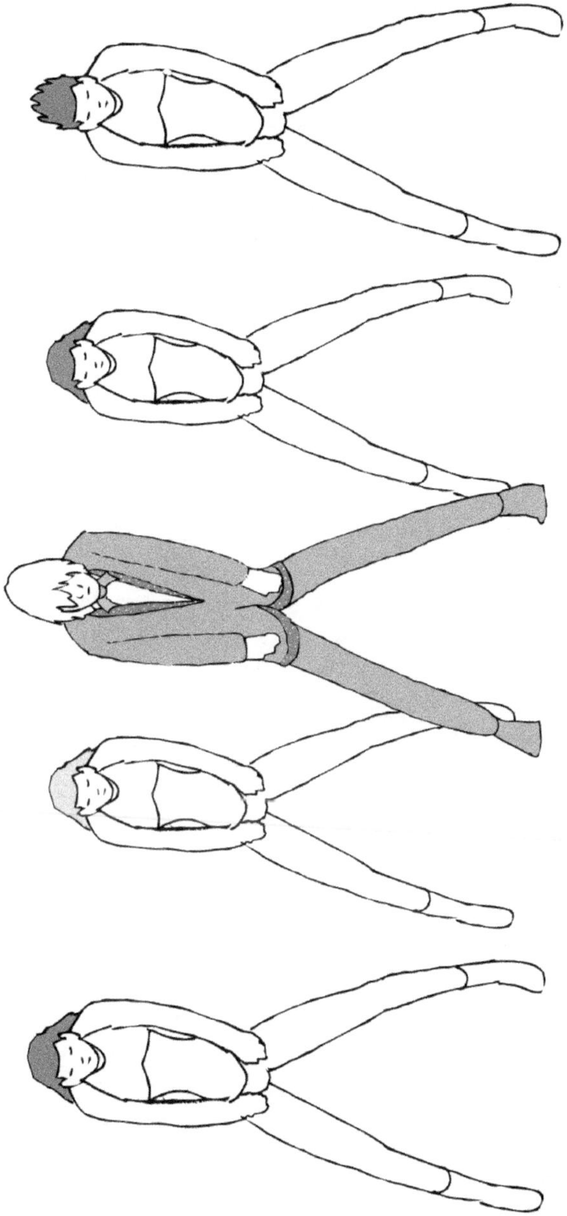

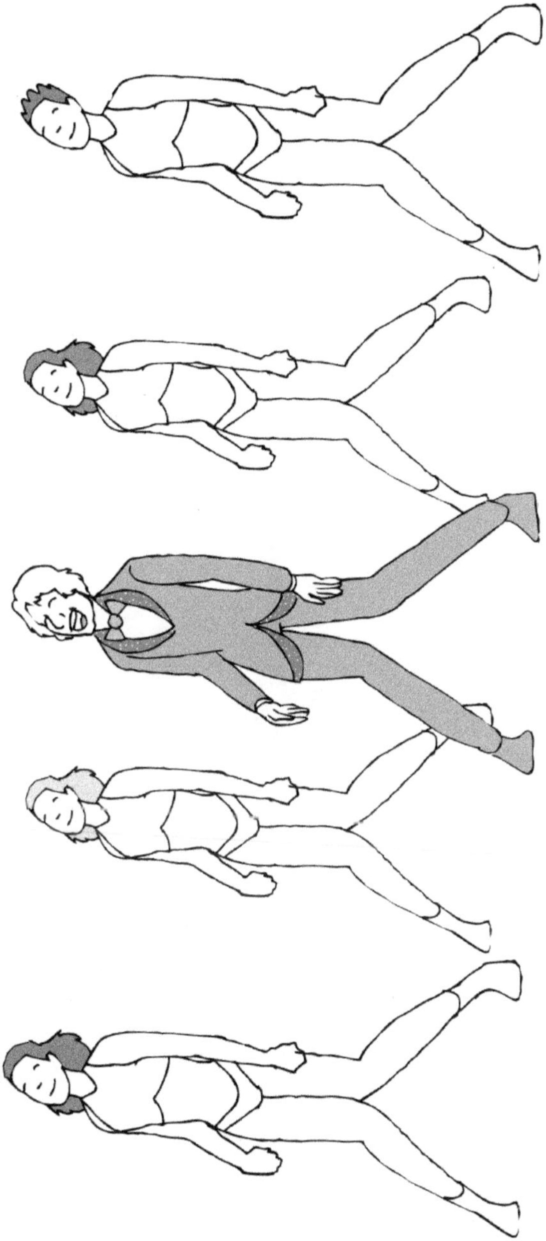

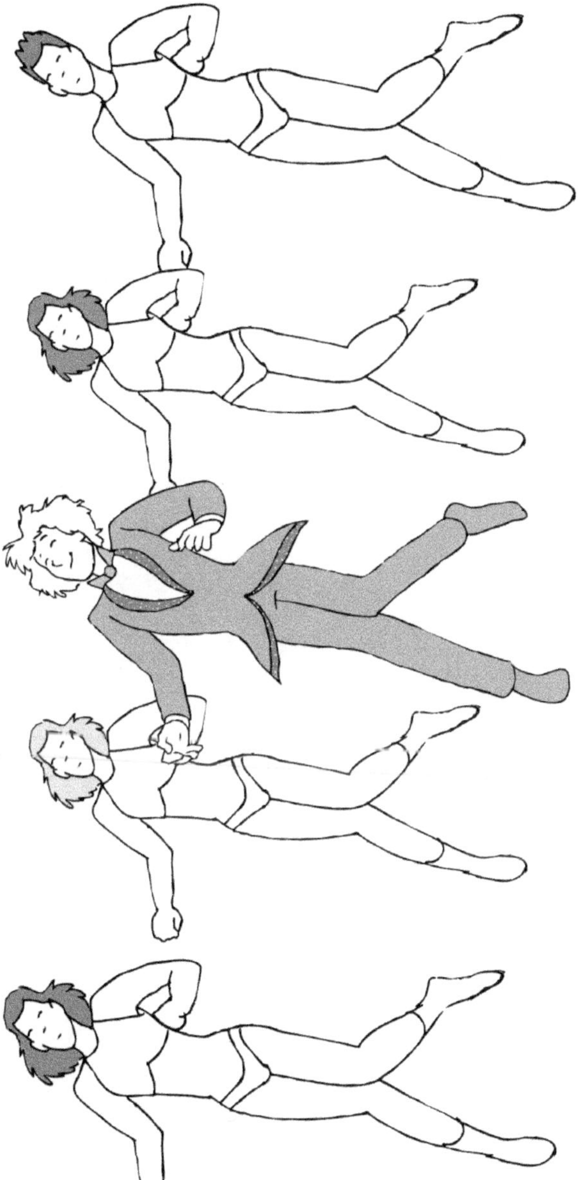

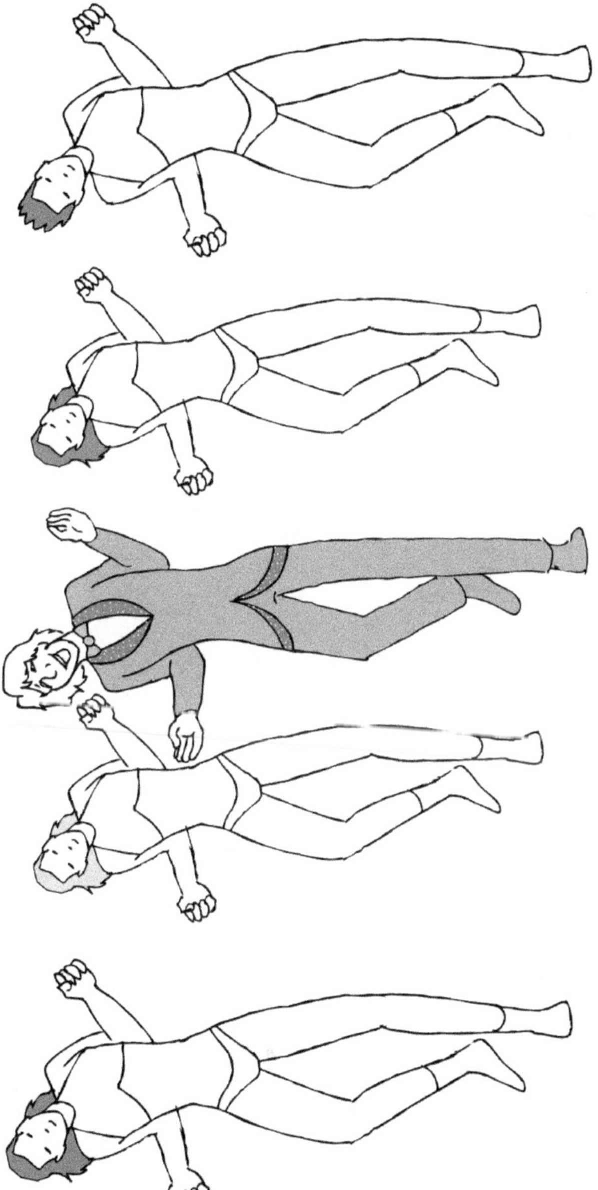

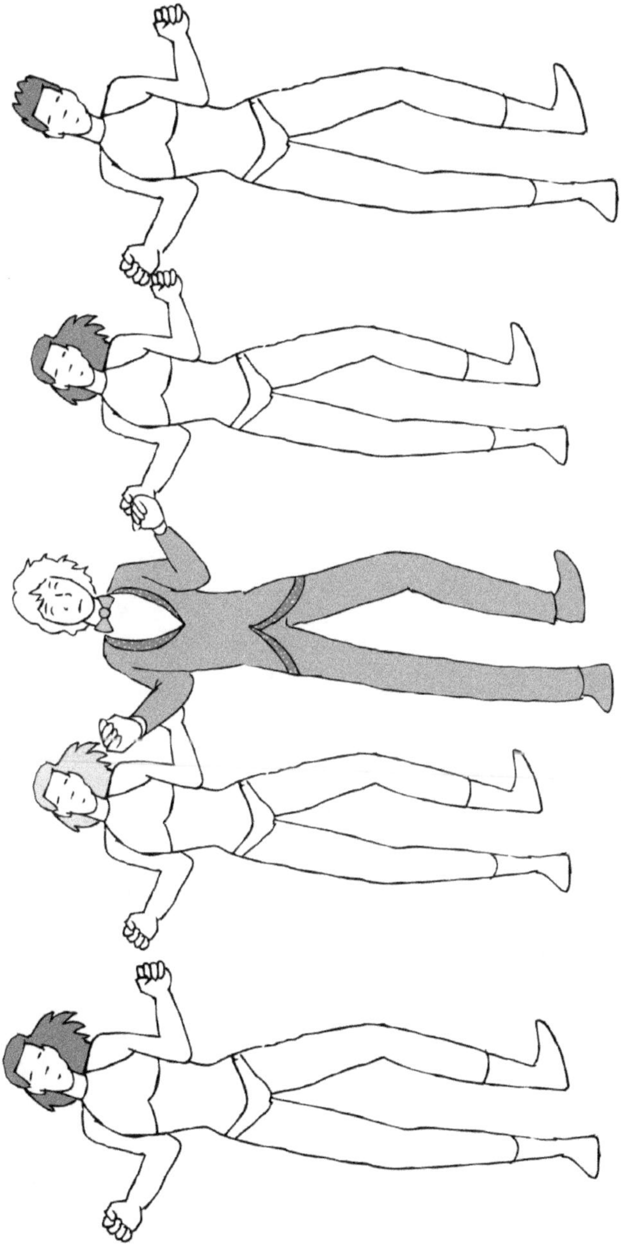

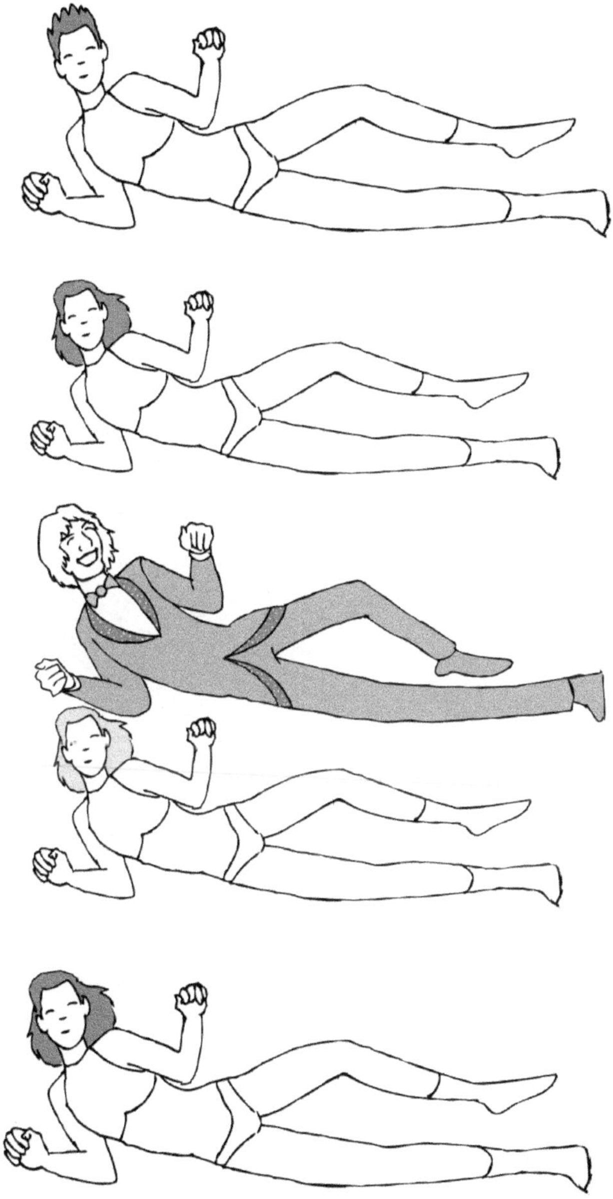

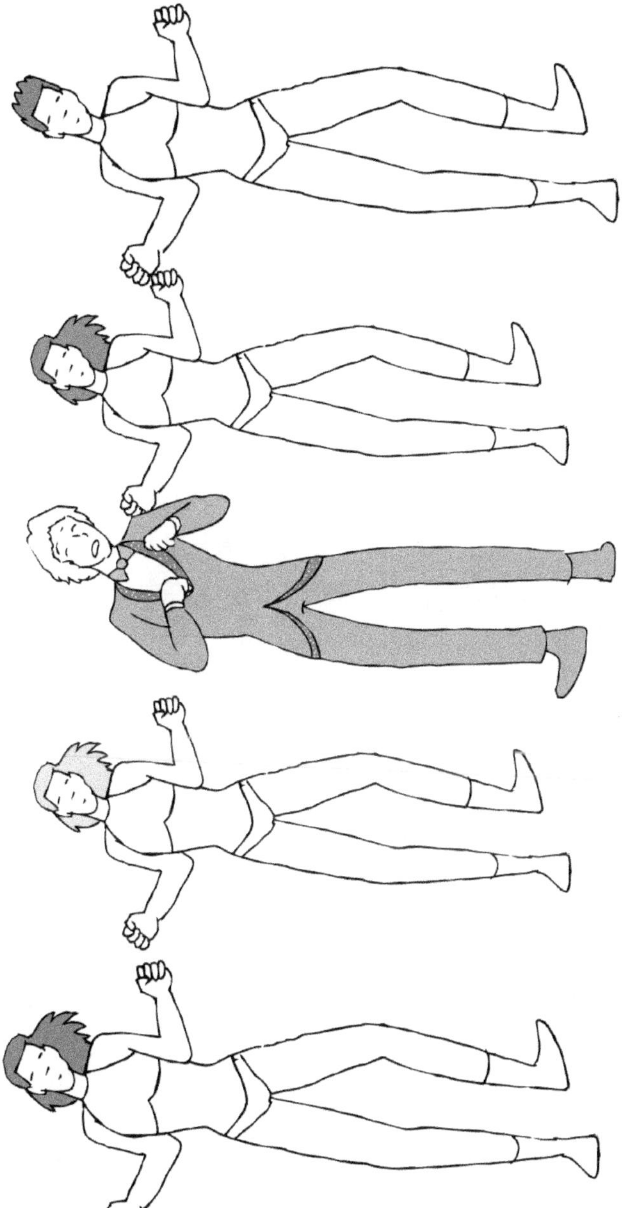

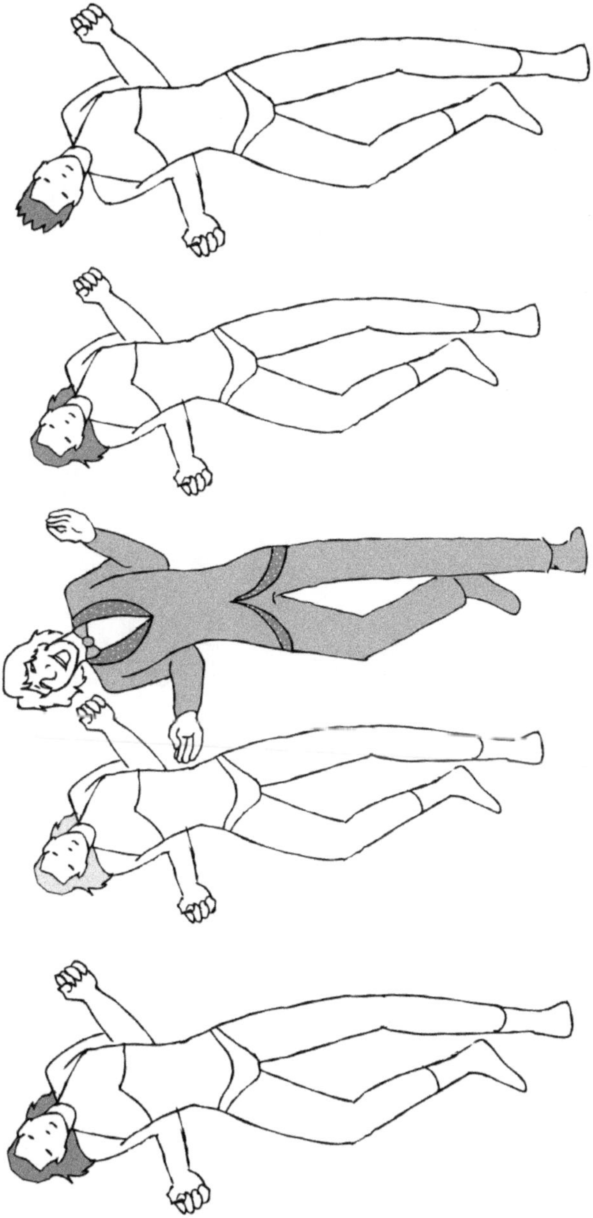

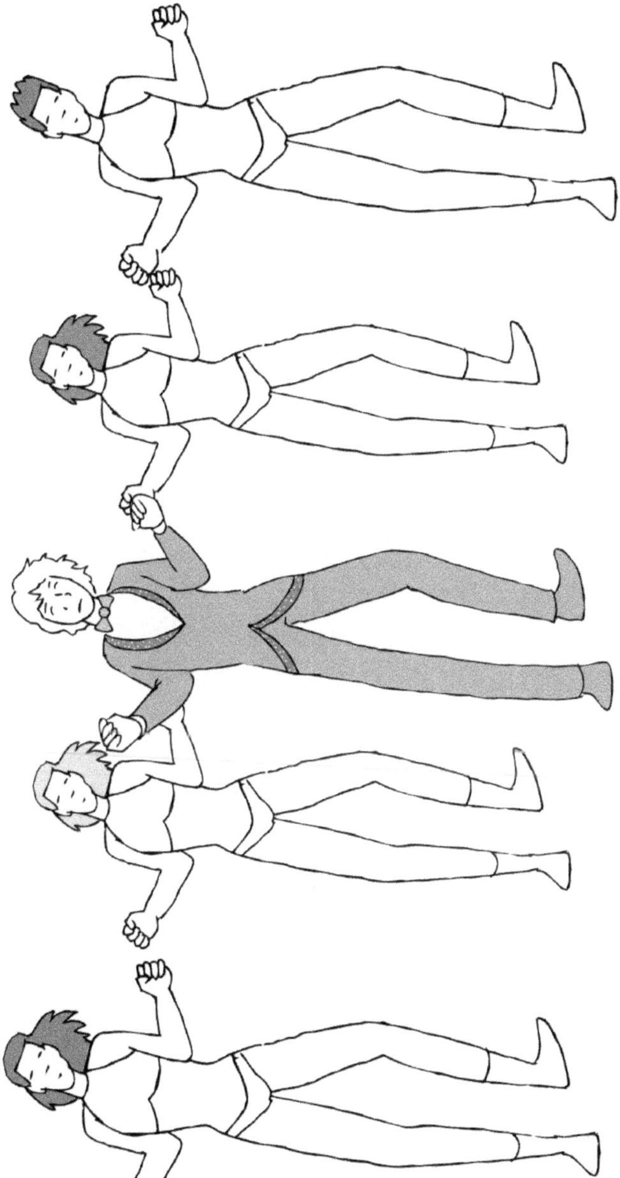

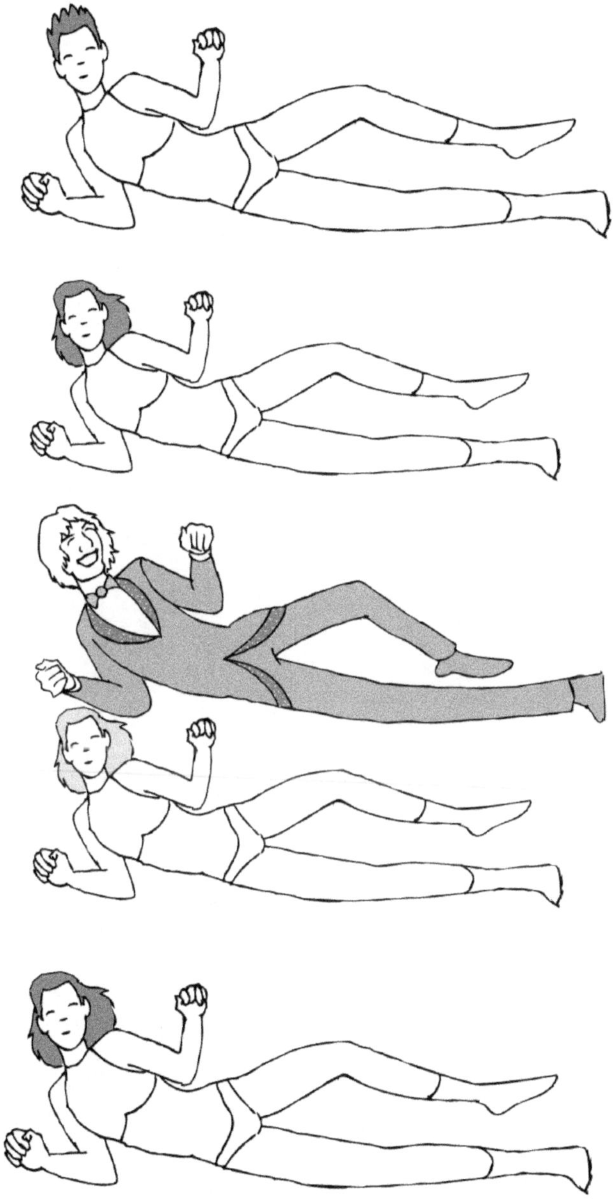

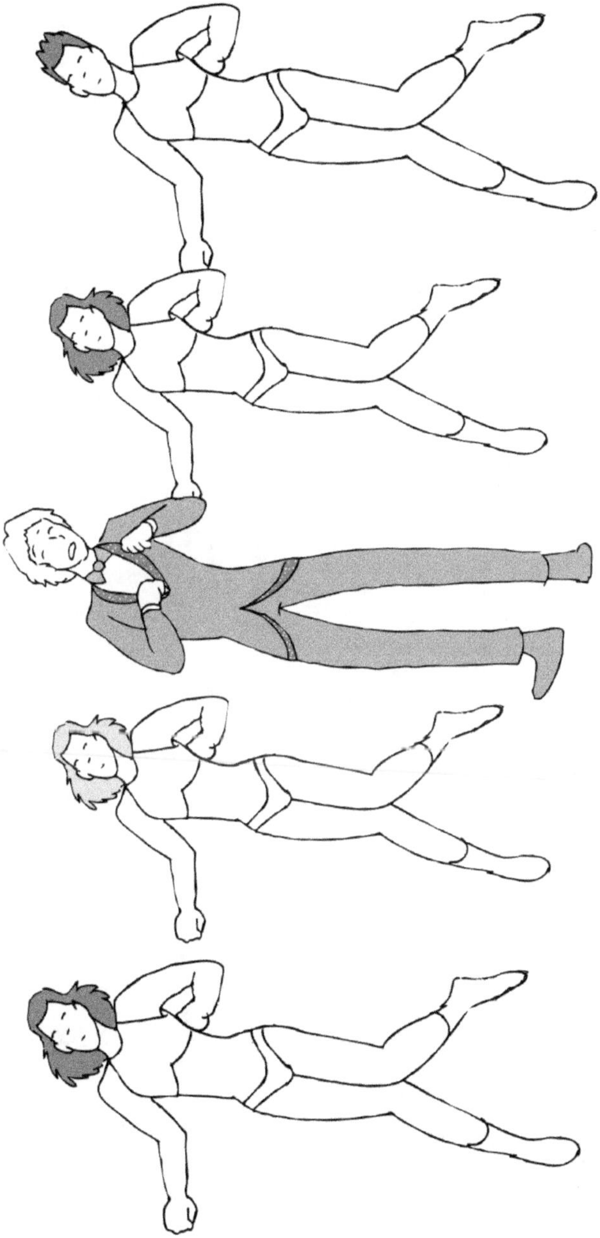

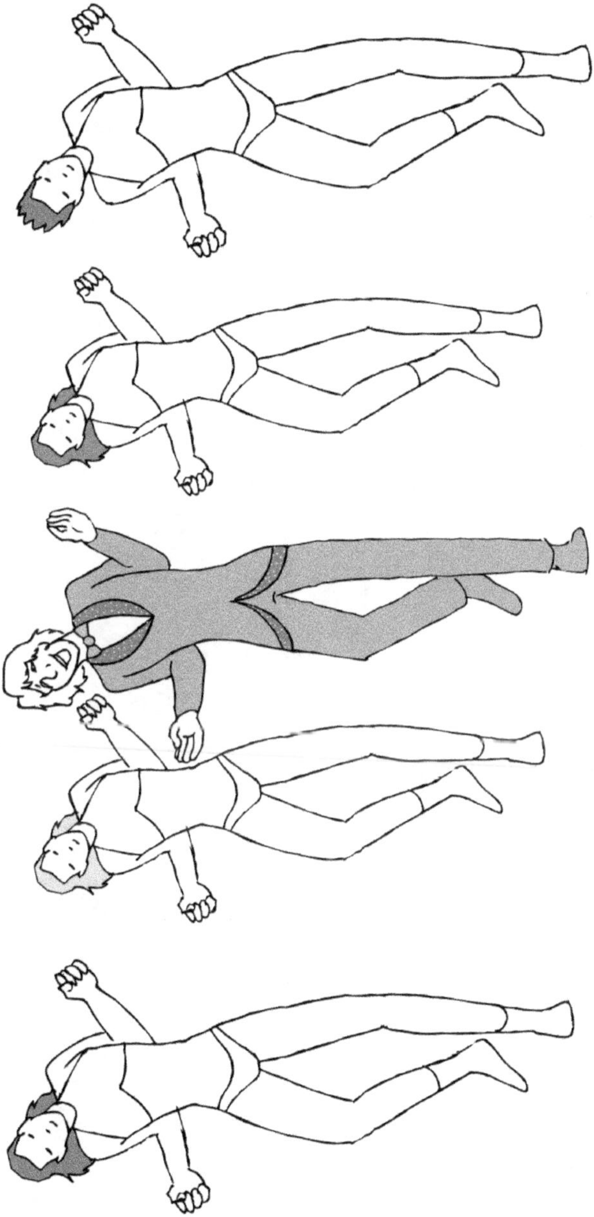

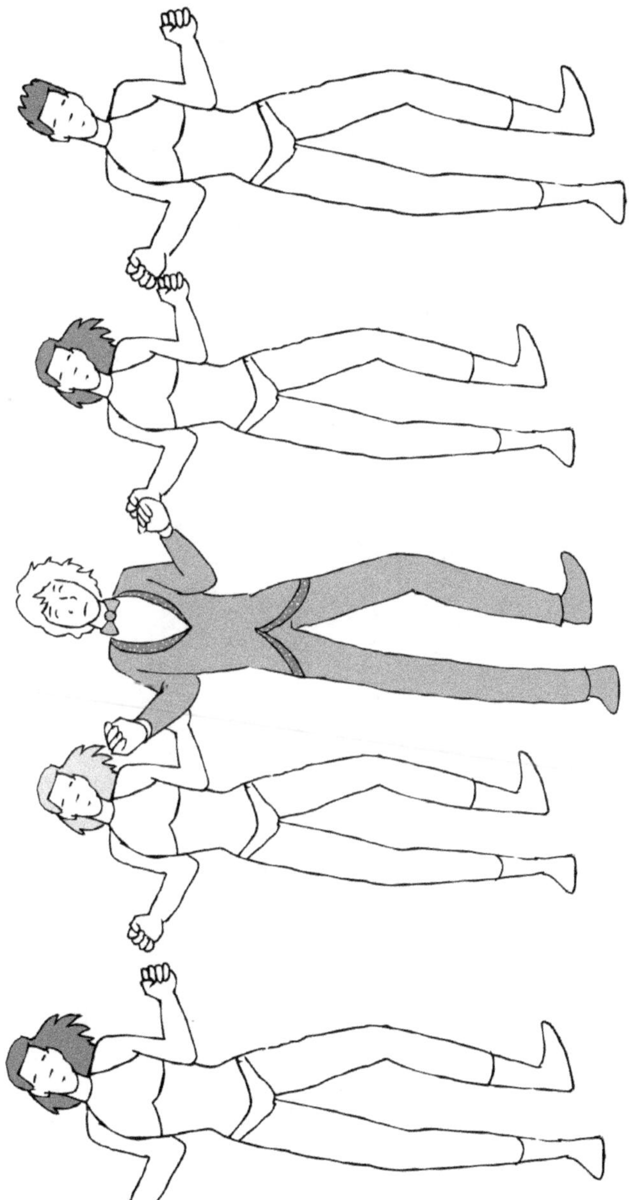

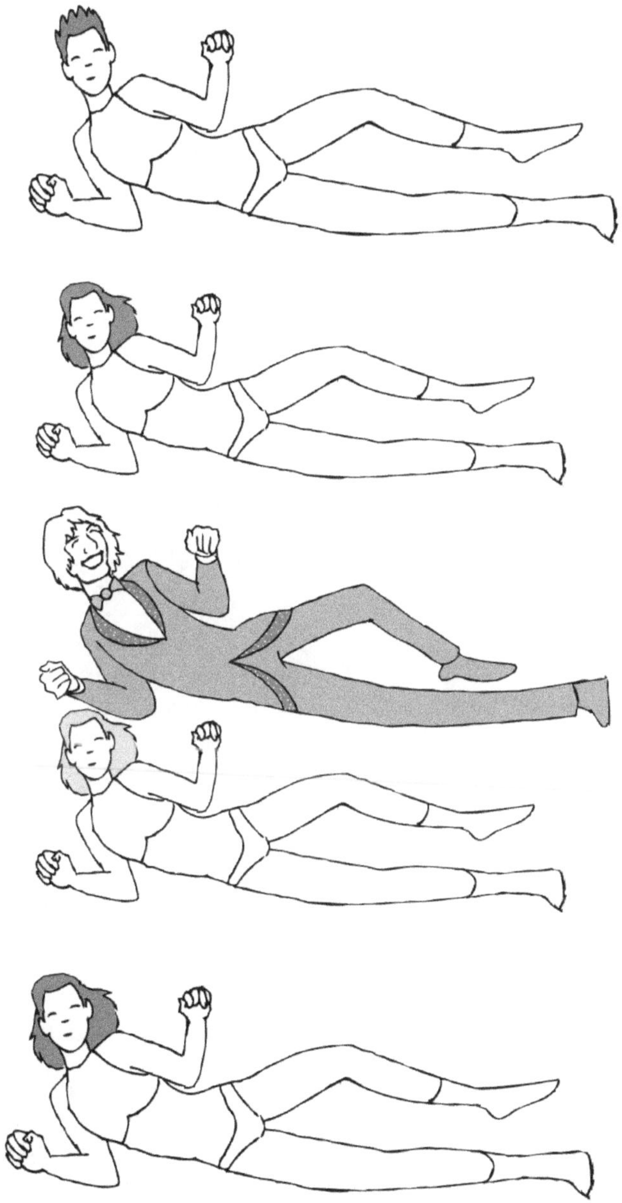

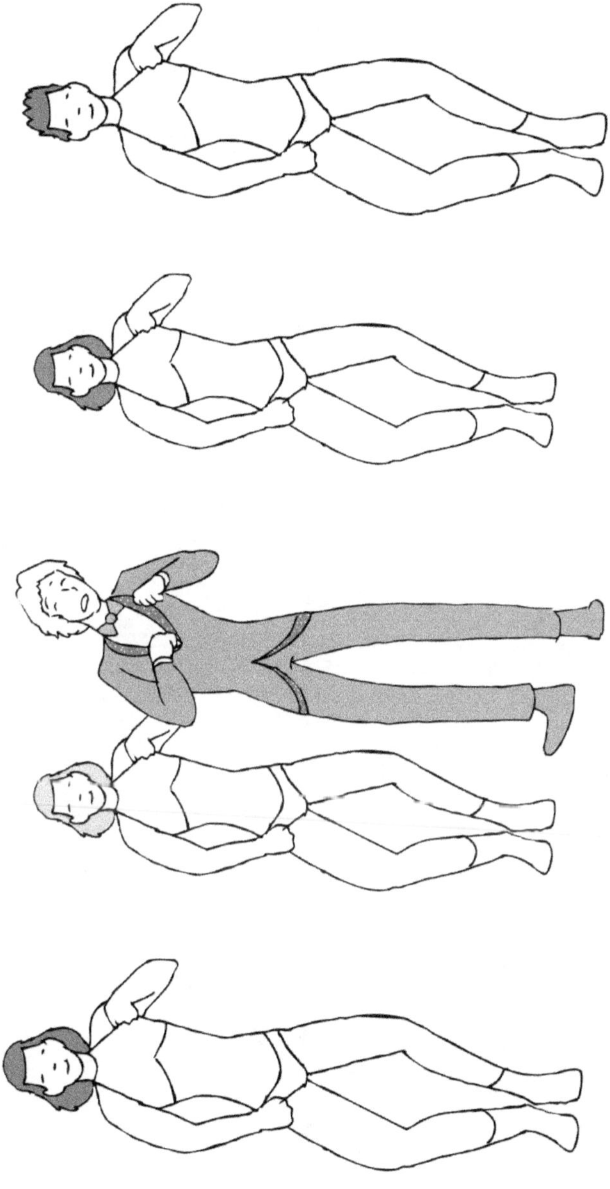

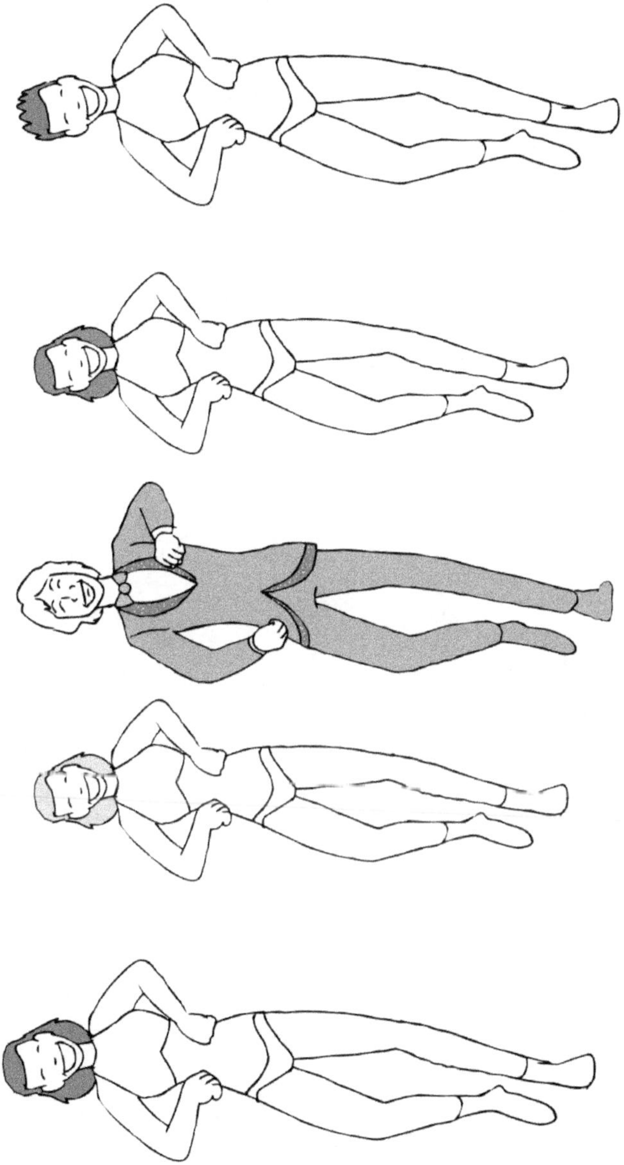

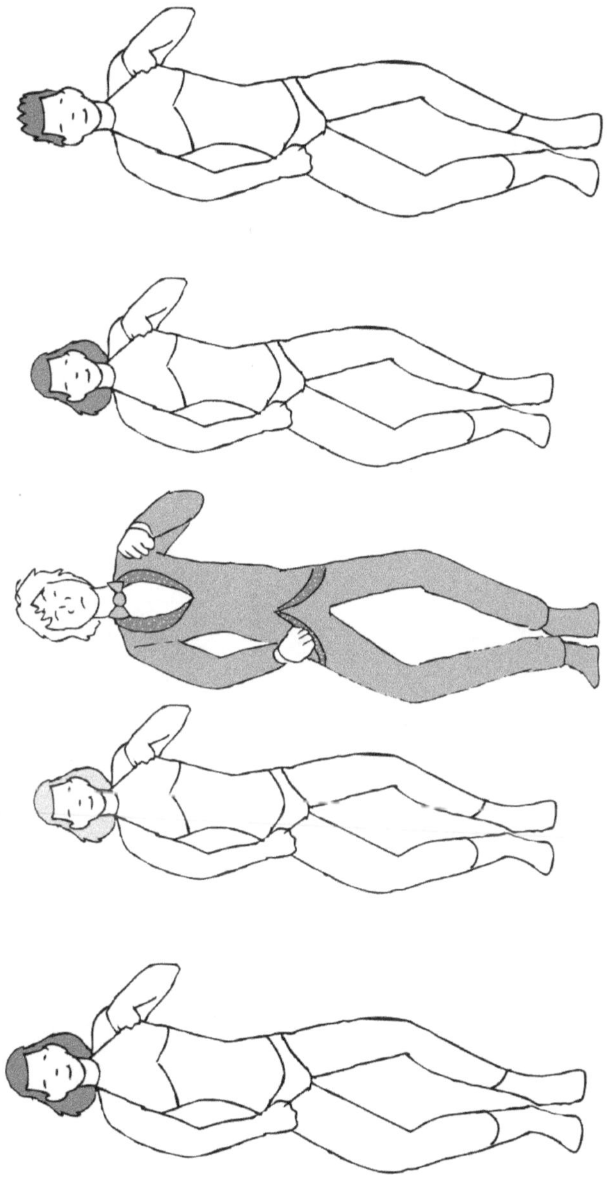

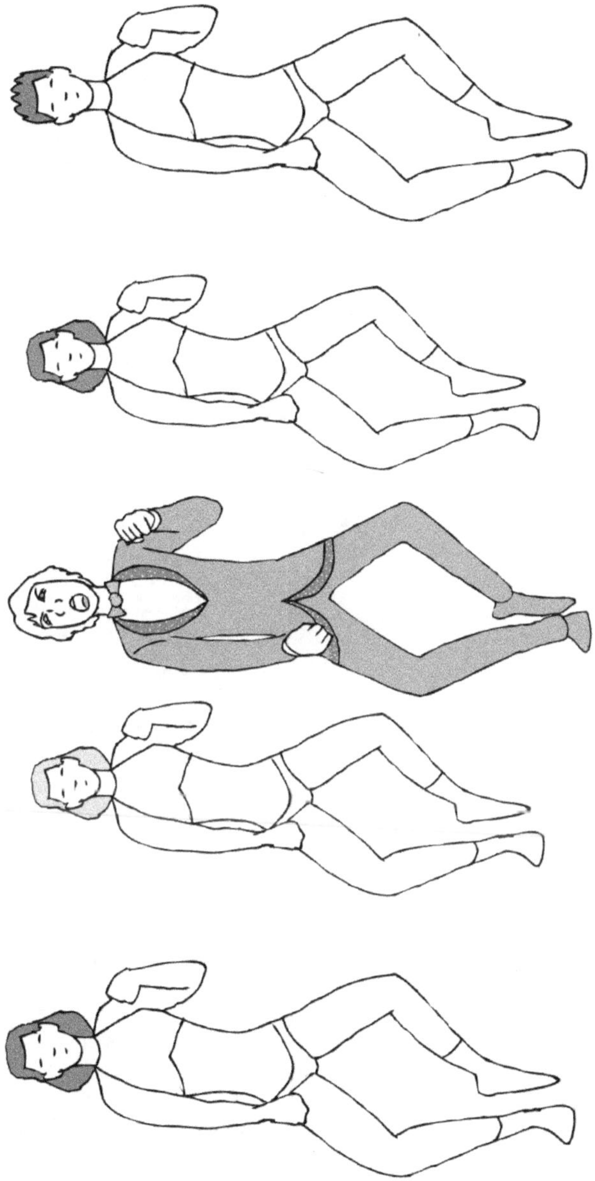

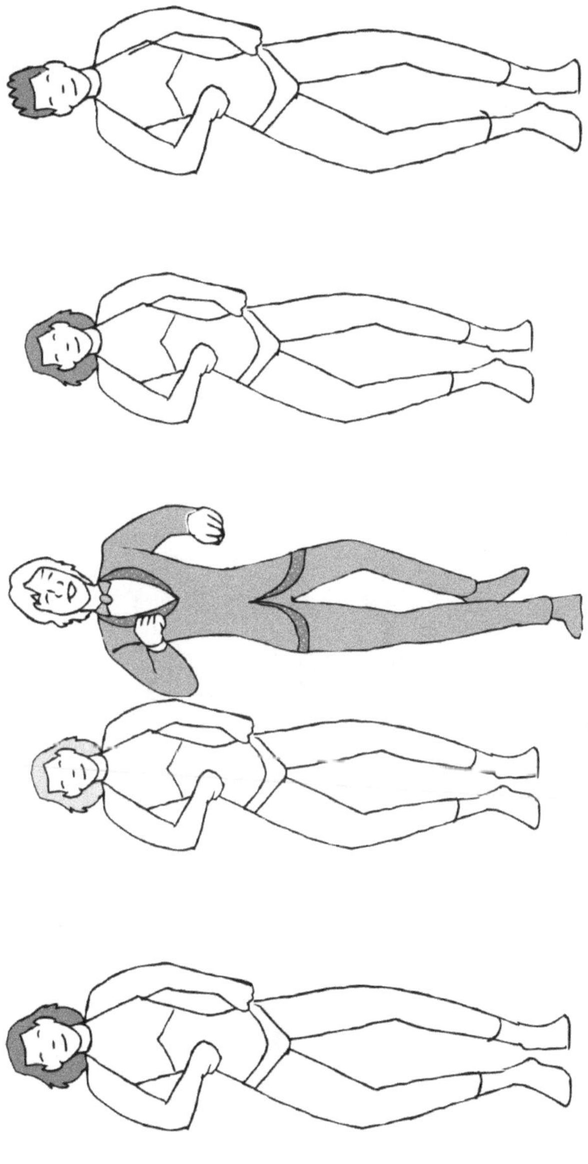

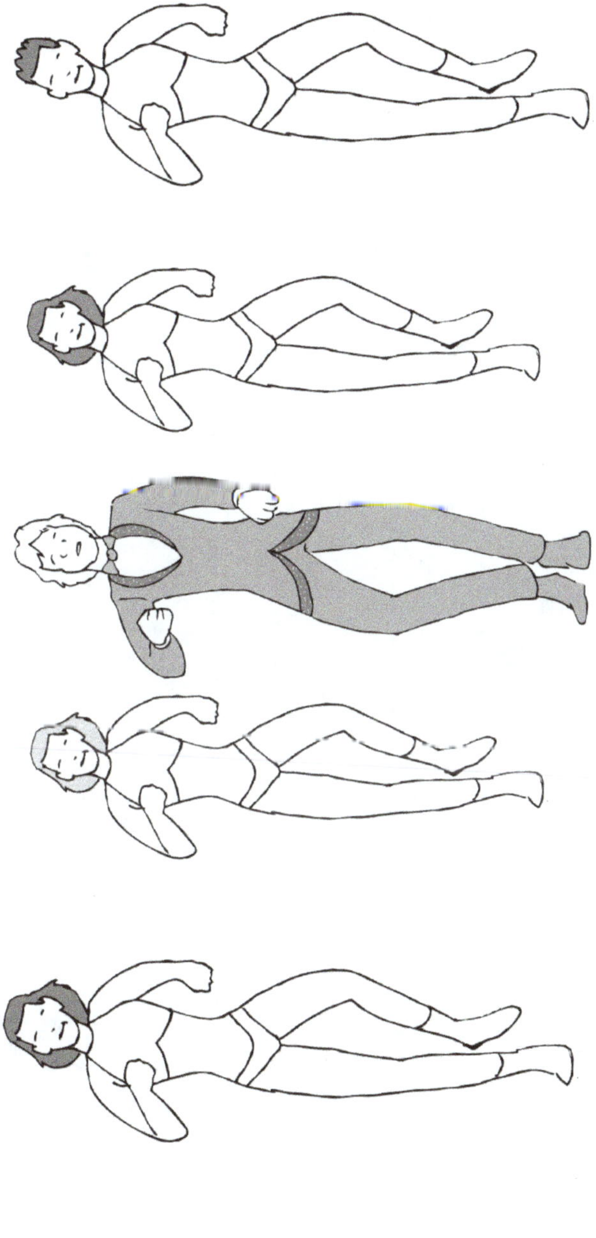

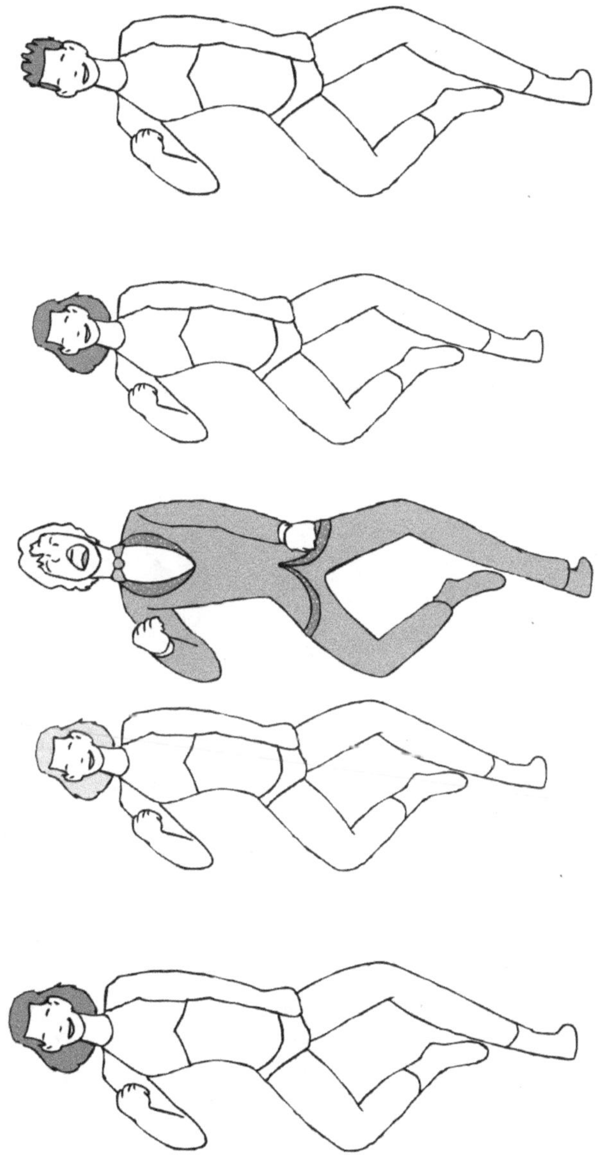

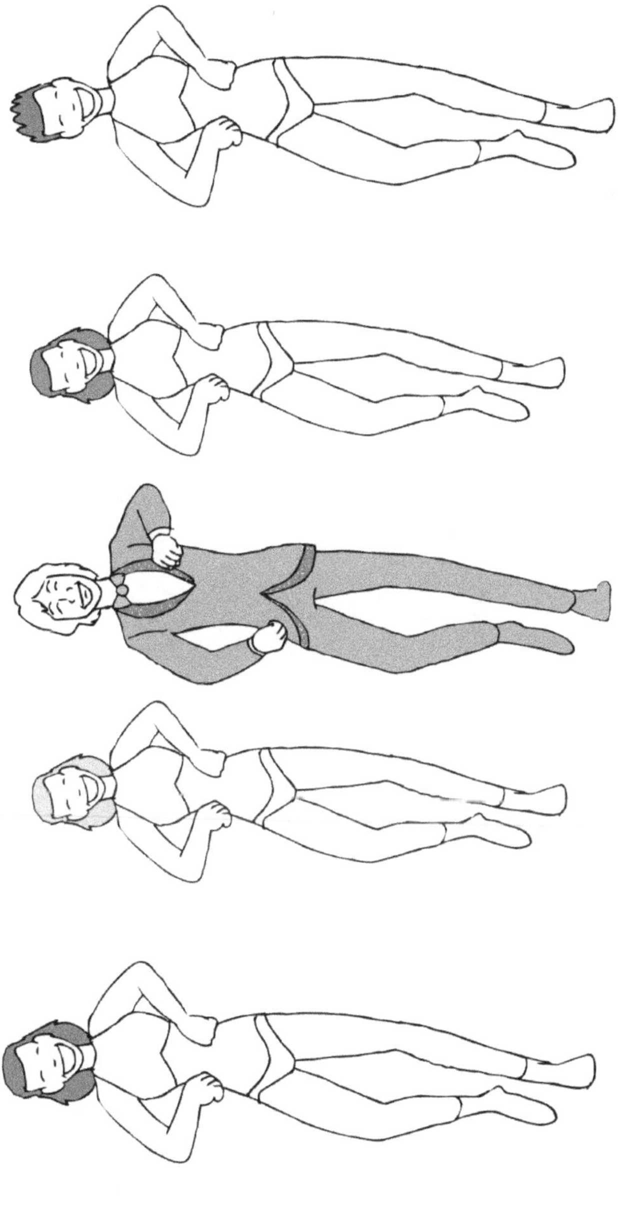

www.ingramcontent.com/pod-product-compliance
Lightning Source LLC
Chambersburg PA
CBHW061220180526
45170CB00003B/1091
* 9 7 8 0 2 4 4 9 9 4 1 0 5 *